Hello!
I am a tortoise.

I0115062

Tortoises are known for their strong sense of smell and good eyesight.

Tortoises have ears, but they do not hear well.

What?

Tortoises don't have teeth.

No need to brush.

I use my "beak-like" mouth to tear off and chew my food.

Tortoises are "herbivores". That means they mainly eat plants like grasses, leaves, and even cactuses.

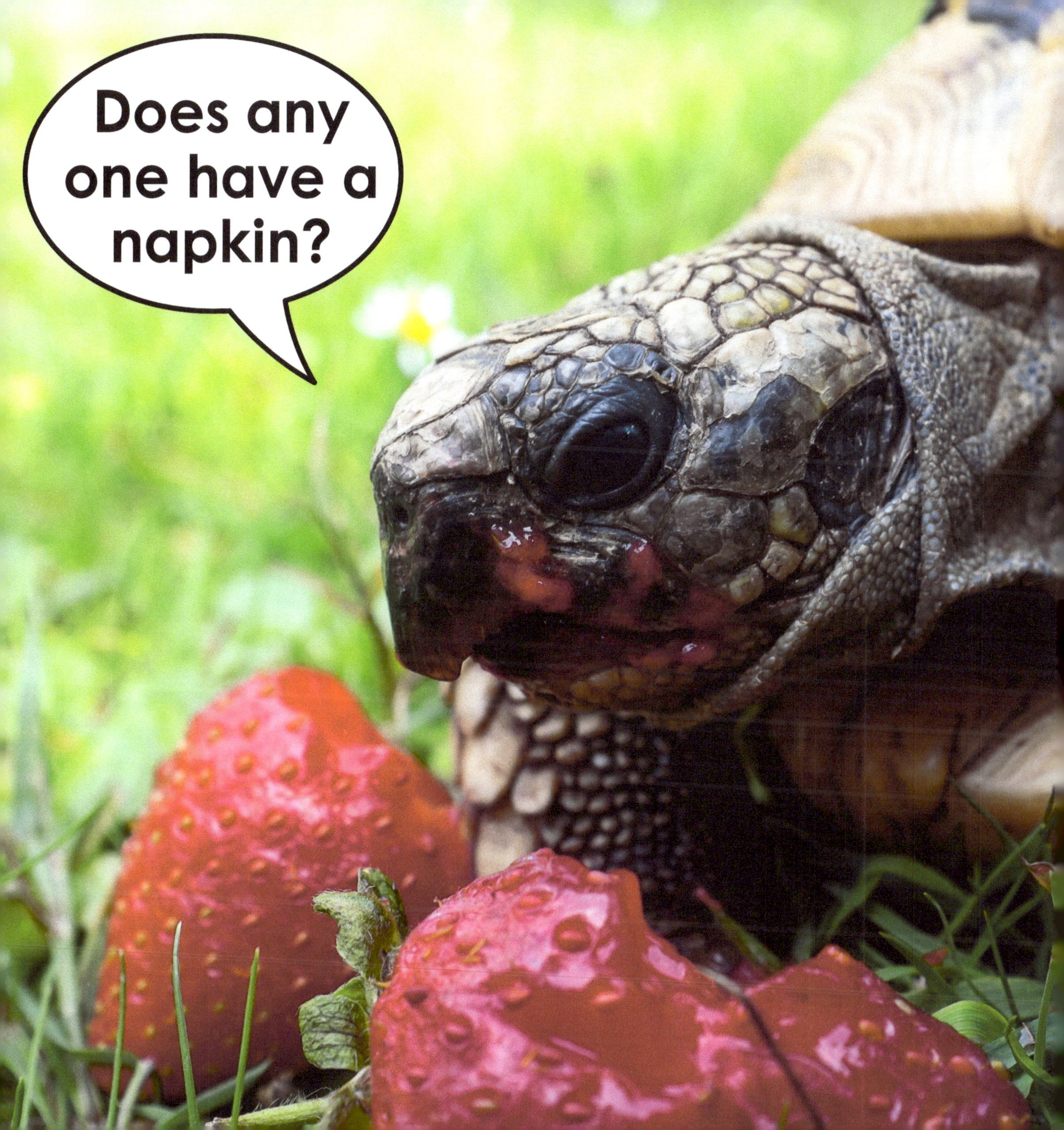
Does any one have a napkin?

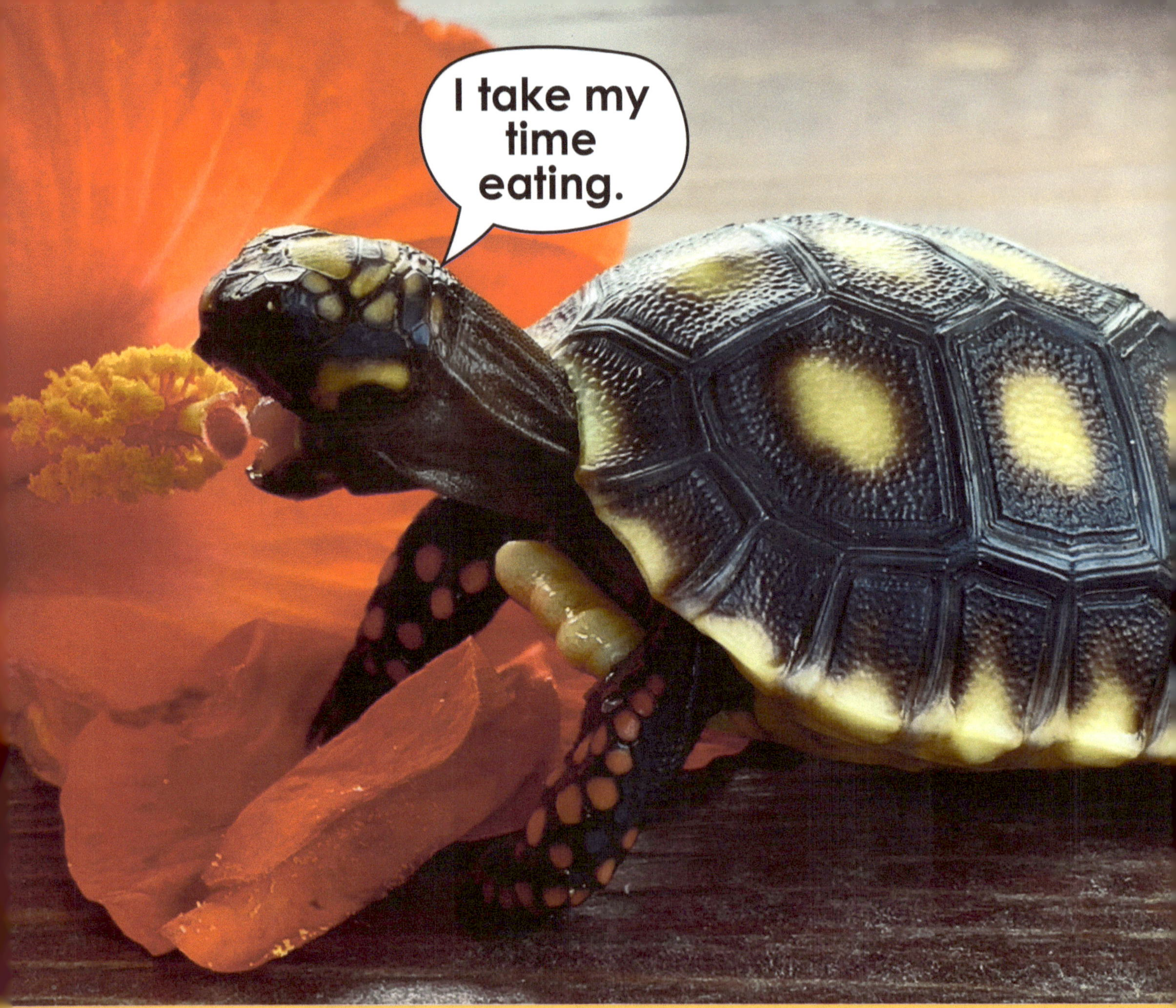

Tortoises may spend hours nibbling on plants and leaves.

When young tortoises feed in groups, they eat much faster, like they are in a race.

I'm a terrible swimmer.

Most tortoises are "terrestrial creatures". That means they stay on the land away from water.

A tortoise's big, heavy shell makes them sink in deep water.

Water is for drinking.

Some tortoises can live for a very long time, with some species reaching over 100 years old.

Hey there, youngster.

I keep getting bigger and bigger and bigger and bigger.

Unlike some animals that stop growing after reaching a certain age, tortoises continue to grow throughout their lives.

The shell of a tortoise is made of bone covered with a layer of "keratin".

Keratin is the same substance that makes up human fingernails and hair.

Each tortoise shell is unique because of type, nutrition and environment.

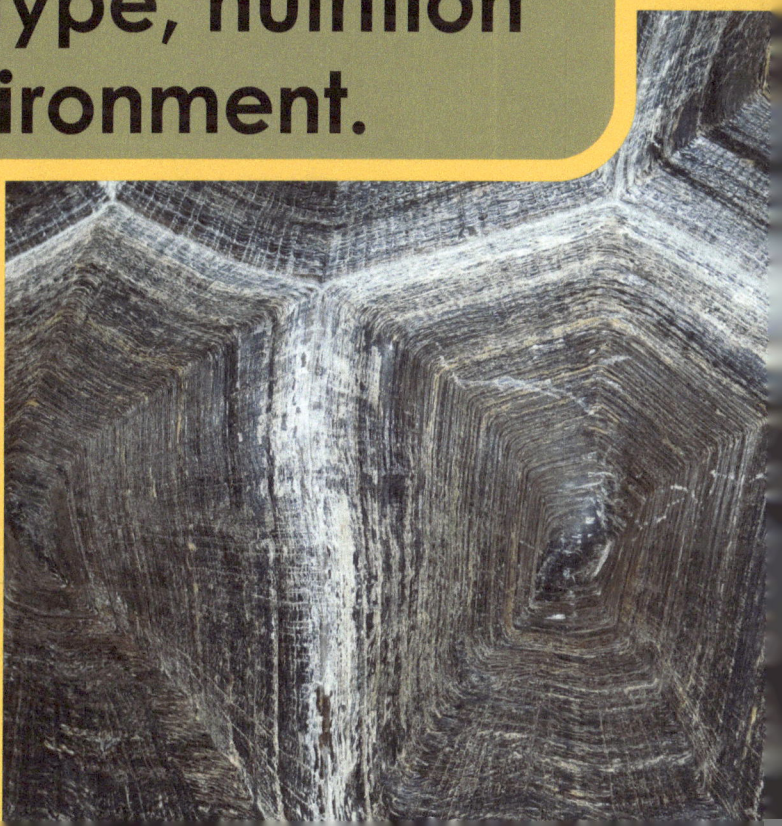

Tortoises can pull their limbs and head into their shell for protection.

I'm safe in here.

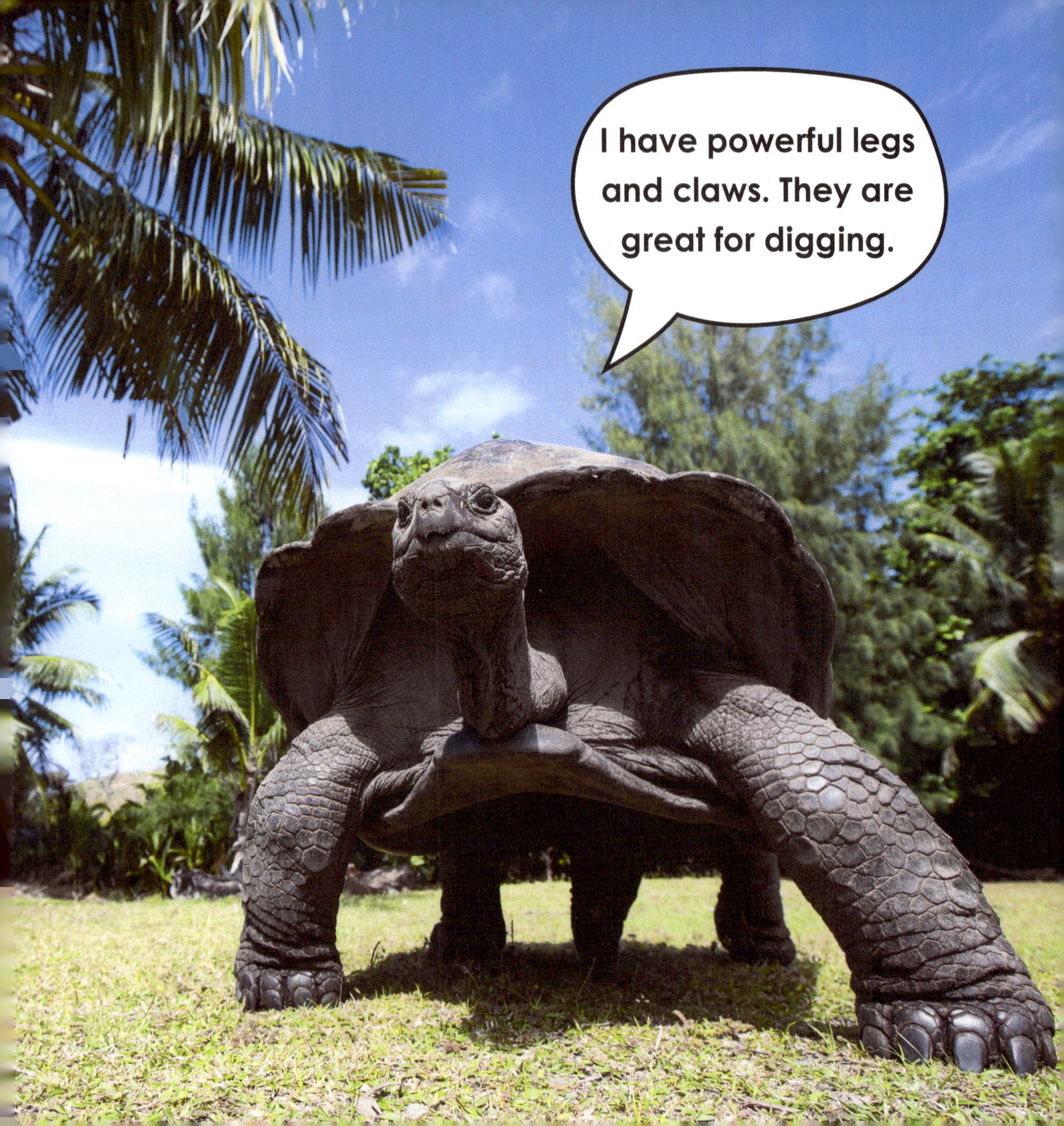
I have powerful legs and claws. They are great for digging.

Some tortoise species live in burrows, which provide protection and insulation from extreme temperatures.

I can store the sun's heat for later.

A tortoise shell absorbs and stores heat and then sends it into the tortoise's body, helping to control body temperature.

Tortoises are "cold-blooded" animals.

That means my body temperature changes with the environment.

Tortoises move very slowly, and their walking speed is usually less than 1 mile per hour.

Taking my time.

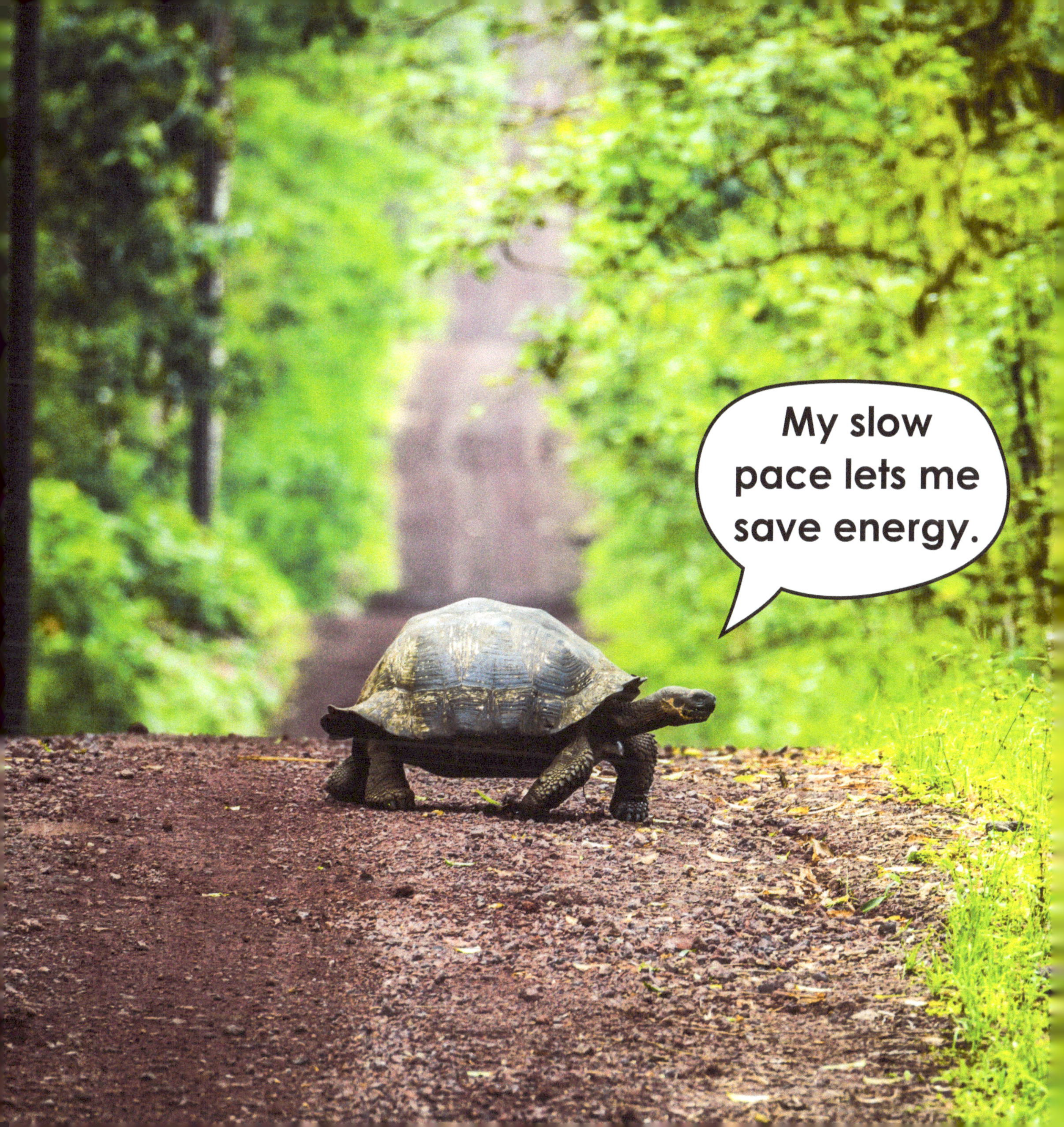
My slow pace lets me save energy.

Tortoises communicate through hisses, grunts, and even head-nodding gestures.

Tortoises are solitary animals and prefer to be alone. However, they do come together for mating.

Care to join me for a slow walk?

Grunt

Get outta here!

When two male tortoises encounter each other within their territories, they can engage in combative behavior.

When tortoises fight they try head-butting or attempting to flip each other over.

Gotcha!

Baby tortoises are called "hatchlings".

That's because we "hatch" from eggs.

As soon as tortoises hatch they instinctively begin searching for food.

Alright, where's breakfast?

We're on our own guys.

Tortoise hatchlings do not receive care from their parents and must fend for themselves.

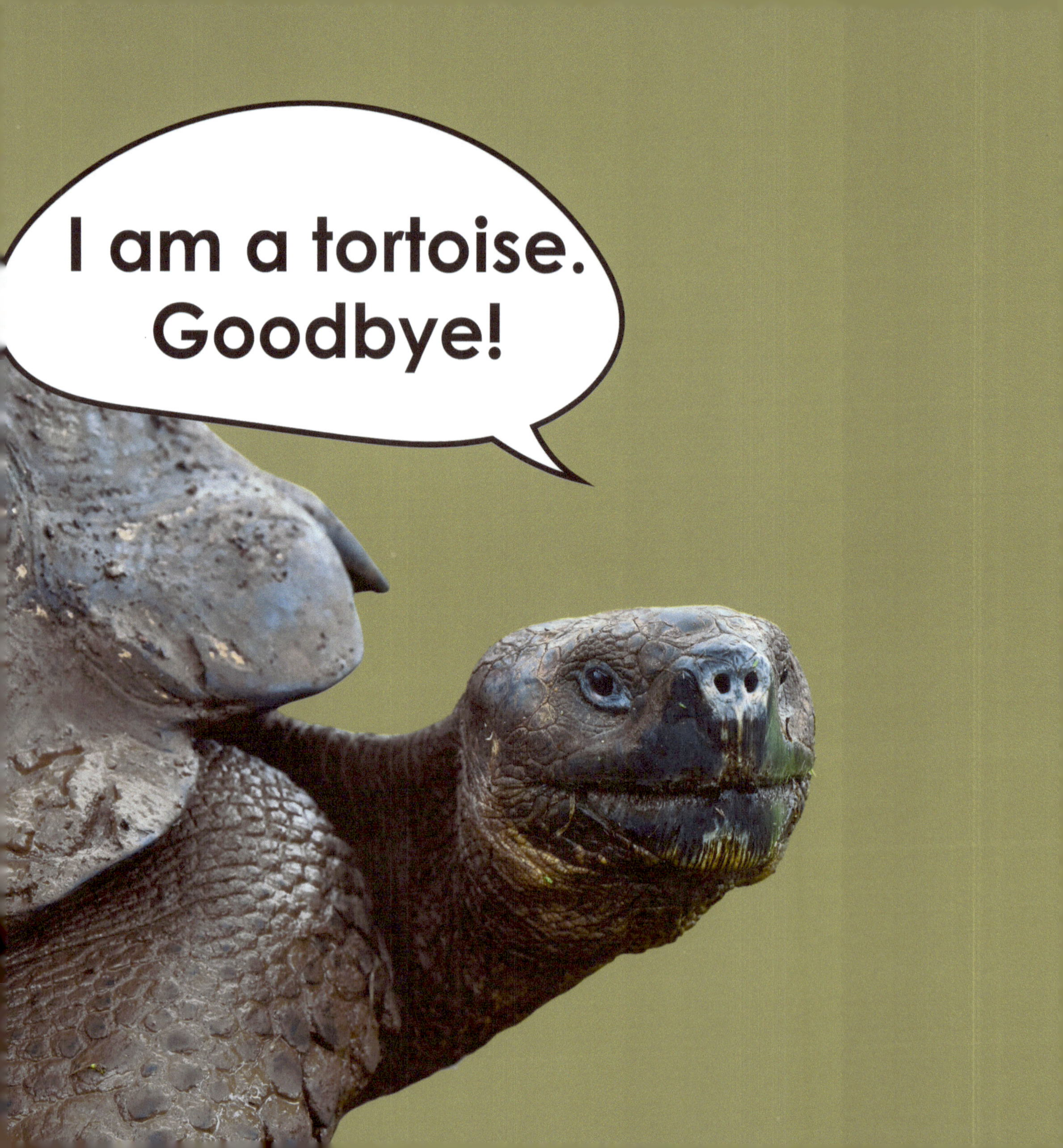
I am a tortoise.
Goodbye!

Want more?

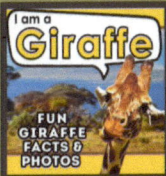      

     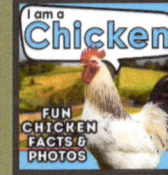 

   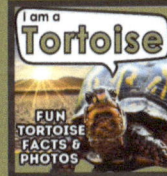  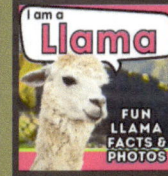 

... and more

COLLECT THEM ALL!

ActiveBrainsBooks.com

Hello parents!

scan here

Visit us to find out about new releases and *FREE* offers. We'll let you know when we have a new release coming out and how you can get it for FREE.
And you can cast your vote for what book we make next!

ActiveBrainsBooks.com

or visit here

---

scan here

Let us know what you think. As an independent publisher, your honest reviews mean a lot to us and our business. We'd love to hear from you!

amazon.com/review/create-review/

or visit here

FOLLOW US on Amazon.

amazon.com/author/activebrainsbooks

ActiveBrainsBooks.com

ACTIVE BRAINS

www.ingramcontent.com/pod-product-compliance
Lightning Source LLC
Chambersburg PA
CBHW060844270326
41933CB00003B/194